CREATURES
OF THE OCEAN

**Michael Leach
and Meriel Lland**

Enslow Publishing
101 W. 23rd Street
Suite 240
New York, NY 10011
USA
enslow.com

This edition published in 2020 by Enslow Publishing, LLC
101 W. 23rd Street, Suite 240, New York, NY 10011

Cataloging-in-Publication Data

Names: Leach, Michael. | Lland, Meriel.
Title: Creatures of the ocean / Michael Leach and Meriel Lland.
Description: New York : Enslow Publishing, 2020. | Series: Animal explorers | Includes bibliographical references and index.
Identifiers: ISBN 9781978509795 (library bound) | ISBN 9781978509771 (pbk.) | ISBN 9781978509788 (6 pack)
Subjects: LCSH: Marine animals—Juvenile literature.
Classification: LCC QL122.2 L43 2020 | DDC 591.77—dc23

Printed in the United States of America

To Our Readers: We have done our best to make sure all website addresses in this book were active and appropriate when we went to press. However, the author and the publisher have no control over and assume no liability for the material available on those websites or on any websites they may link to. Any comments or suggestions can be sent by email to customerservice@enslow.com.

Photo Credits:
Every attempt has been made to clear copyright. Should there be any inadvertent omission, please apply to the publisher for rectification.

Key: b-bottom, t-top, c-center, l-left, r-right

Alamy: 4–5 (Ian Cruickshank), 8b (Norbert Probst/Imagebroker), 12–13 (Imagebroker), 13br (Richard Hermann/ Minden Pictures), 16–17 (Scott Leslie/Minden Pictures), 18–19 (Reinhard Dirscherl), 18c (Reinhard Dirscherl), 19b & 31bl (Reinhard Dirscherl), 20tr (Norbert Wu/Minden Pictures), 20cl (Photo Researchers), 21 (Norbert Wu/Minden Pictures), 24cl (Photo Researchers); Alex Hindle: 22–23; Shutterstock: cover and title page; 4cl (Puwadol Jaturawutthichai), 4br (Alen thien), 5tr (Giedrilius), 5cl (David Bokuchava), 5br (Dennis van de Water), 6cl (Ethan Daniels), 6br daulon), 7br (Lebendkulturen.de), 8–9 (Damsea), 8c (Aries Sutanto), 9br (Juncat), 10–11 (wildestanimal), 10cl (Grant M Henderson), 11tr (Adisom Chaikit), 11br (Voinau Pavel), 12c (pr2is) 12br (Voinau Pavel), 14–15 (Kjersti Joergensen), 14cl (Vladimir Wrangel), 15br (Bonezboyz), 17tr & 32br (Dudarev Mikhail), 17cl & 31br (Rayto), 17br (Arkadivna), 18br (Val_Iva), 20br (Rhoeo), 22cr (Dewald Kirsten), 22b (stefanphotozemun), 23br (VectorPot), 24–25 (aquapix), 24br (Vectorpocket), 25br (tae208), 26tr (wildestanimal), 26tl (Mohamed AlQubaisi), 26cr (Al-Tair), 26bl (Kletr), 27tl (small1), 27tr (Brian Kinney), 27cl (best works), 27br (chonlasub woravichan), 27bl (aquapix), 28cr (Vladimir Wrangel), 29tr (Andrey Luzhanskiy), 29bl (olgalngs); Wikimedia Commons: 26br (Will Thomas).

CONTENTS

Introduction

An animal is a living organism made up of cells. It feeds, senses, and responds to its surroundings, moves, and reproduces. Scientists have identified nearly nine million species of living animals, but there are many more to be found.

Rhinoceros hornbills are birds that live in Southeast Asian rain forests. Birds are warm-blooded animals with backbones. They have wings and most can fly.

Life Appears

Single-celled life forms appeared around four billion years ago. Sponges—the first animals—appeared a billion years ago. Over time, more complicated animals evolved and some also became extinct. Dinosaurs were the dominant land animals for 165 million years before they died out 65 million years ago.

Fossilized skull of the dinosaur *Tyrannosaurus rex*

Leaf beetle, an insect

Classifying Life

Scientists organize living things into groups with shared characteristics. The two main kinds of animal are ones with backbones (vertebrates) and ones without (invertebrates). Arthropods make up the biggest invertebrate group. They have segmented bodies and jointed limbs. Insects, spiders, and crabs are all arthropods.

Warm- and Cold-Blooded

Most animals are ectothermic, or "cold-blooded." Their body temperature is controlled by their environment. Mammals and birds are endothermic, or "warm-blooded." Their bodies can generate their own heat, so they can survive in much colder habitats.

Musk ox, a mammal

Langurs in a city

Fragile Earth

We are lucky to share our world with an extraordinary richness of animals. It is important to protect our wildlife. When humans pollute or damage the environment, we harm both animals and people. The future is in our hands.

Giant leaf–tailed gecko, vulnerable because of habitat loss

Animal Habitats

The place where an animal lives is called its habitat. Animals have evolved to inhabit just about every environment on Earth, from tropical rain forests and coral reefs to deserts, mountaintops, and ice floes. They even survive in cities.

Sea Creatures

Water covers more than two-thirds of our planet and the oceans are home to more life than the land. From tiny plankton to the colossal blue whale, animals have adapted to every marine environment. The 650 feet (200 m) closest to the surface, where there is warmth and light from the sun, has most life.

Predators and Prey

Many marine animals survive by eating other species. Some hunt large prey, while others scavenge remains and debris from the seabed. Ocean animals have developed ways to protect themselves from predators.

Many soft-bodied sea creatures are protected by a thick shell. The giant clam shuts its shell if it feels threatened.

GIANT OCEANIC MANTA RAY

MANTA BIROSTRIS
"TWO-NOSED BLANKET"

Habitat: Warm oceans; near the equator
Length: Male 14.8 feet (4.5 m); female 18 feet (5.5 m)
Weight: Male 2,866 pounds (1,300 kg); female 3,527 pounds (1,600 kg)
Diet: Shrimp, krill
Life span: Up to 80 years
Wild population: Unknown; Vulnerable

The body can be up to 23 feet (7 m) wide.

Although they look like underwater birds, manta rays are fish. They feed on some of the smallest life in the sea—tiny invertebrates called plankton.

Microscopic Life

Plankton is a floating soup of tiny plants and animals. Some of the animals are the larvae (young) of jellyfish, crabs, and other invertebrates. Plankton is an important food for many sea creatures, from simple sea sponges to enormous whale sharks and blue whales.

Plankton includes tiny crustaceans called copepods. These two are clearly females because they are carrying sacs of eggs.

Fish

More than half of vertebrates are fish. These cold-blooded animals live in salt or fresh water, have tails and body fins, breathe through gills, and usually have scales. There are around 28,000 species, from the 41.5-foot (12.6 m) whale shark to a tiny swamp carp that measures just 0.3 inches (8 mm).

The parrotfish is named for its beak-like mouth, designed for biting chunks of coral off the reef.

Staying Safe

Many species limit the risk of being eaten by larger fish by sticking together in schools for safety. Other fish have amazing camouflage to avoid being seen. Speed and swimming prowess save the lives of some fish. Others have defensive spines, scales, or toxins.

The puffer fish transforms itself if an enemy appears. It takes in enough water to double in size. The fish is suddenly ball-shaped, and covered with poison-tipped spines.

Extraordinary Eels

Eels look more like snakes than fish. Long and thin, they move by wriggling. Eels are found in the sea and fresh water and most don't have scales. Some species can even move on land. Eels usually spend the day hiding in rocky crevices and come out at night to hunt.

The giant moray eel is a predator that lives on coral reefs. It can grow as long as 9.8 feet (3 m).

At night, the parrotfish covers its body with slimy mucus. This hides its scent from nocturnal hunters.

The fish's gills are behind the cheek flap. They take oxygen from the water and produce waste carbon dioxide.

Moving the tail fin from side to side generates thrust. It propels the fish forward in the water.

STOPLIGHT PARROTFISH

SPARISOMA VIRIDE "GOLDEN-HEADED GREEN FISH"

Habitat: Coral reefs; Western Atlantic
Length: Male 1.6 feet (50 cm); female 1 foot (30 cm)
Weight: Male 3.5 pounds (1.6 kg); female 3.1 pounds (1.4 kg)
Diet: Coral polyps, algae
Life span: Up to 30 years
Wild population: Unknown; Least Concern

Sharks

Sharks are fish with skeletons made of tough, flexible cartilage instead of bone. They first appeared 220 million years before the dinosaurs. Today there are more than 500 species. Sharks have a reputation as fierce predators, but most species are harmless and shark attacks are rare.

All Shapes and Sizes

Most sharks—including the great white, tiger, blue, bull, mako, and reef sharks—have a sleek, streamlined body. Others are very different shapes. In deep waters, the frilled shark is long and eel-like, while the goblin shark is named for its unusual nose. The flattened bodies of angel sharks and wobbegongs suit life on the seabed.

The skin is as rough as sandpaper. It is covered with grooved, tooth-shaped scales that direct the flow of water over the shark's body and reduce drag.

The great white has an excellent sense of taste. It can detect a few drops of blood in the water from 3 miles (5 km) away.

The shark has rows of sharp, triangular teeth up to 3 inches (7.6 cm) long. As old ones are lost, new teeth move forward to take their place.

There are ten species of hammerhead shark. These have a T-shaped head with eyes far apart, which gives them a wide field of vision.

A torpedo-shaped body, pointed at each end, cuts down water resistance. The shark swims at 25 miles (40 km) per hour.

Filter Feeders

The three largest shark species— the whale shark, basking shark, and megamouth—do not hunt large prey. They take in water through their enormous, gaping mouths, and then force it out again through their gills. Their filter pads capture microscopic plants and animals from the water.

A whale shark's mouth is 4.9 feet (1.5 m) wide. It contains more than 300 rows of tiny teeth and ten filter pads for sieving plankton from seawater.

GREAT WHITE SHARK

CARCHARODON CARCHARIAS "POINTED TOOTH"

Habitat: Oceans worldwide except the poles
Length: Male 13.1 feet (4 m); female 14.8 feet (4.5 m)
Weight: Male 1,764 pounds (800 kg); female 2,205 pounds (1,000 kg)
Diet: Fish including sharks, turtles, marine mammals
Life span: Up to 70 years
Wild population: Unknown; Vulnerable

Cephalopods

Octopuses, squid, cuttlefish, and nautiluses belong to a group of animals called cephalopods ("head-foots"). Cephalopods have a large head, big brain, and a set of arms for gathering food. There are around 800 species. The nautilus is the only living cephalopod with a shell.

The octopus's head lies between the arms and body. It has well-developed eyes, a large brain, and a beak-like mouth. The octopus's poisonous saliva paralyzes prey.

Close Cousins

Octopuses and squid both have eight arms, but the squid also has a pair of tentacles that it uses to grab prey. Many octopuses spend their time on the seabed, where they eat crabs, clams, limpets, and scallops. Squid live in the open ocean and hunt fish, crustaceans, and other squid.

The giant Pacific octopus can change its reddish-brown skin to blend in with its surroundings.

COMMON OCTOPUS

OCTOPUS VULGARIS
"COMMON EIGHT FOOT"

Habitat: Warm oceans worldwide
Length: 2 feet (60 cm)
Weight: 12.1 pounds (5.5 kg)
Diet: Fish, mollusks, crabs, other marine invertebrates
Life span: Up to 18 months
Wild population: Unknown; Least Concern

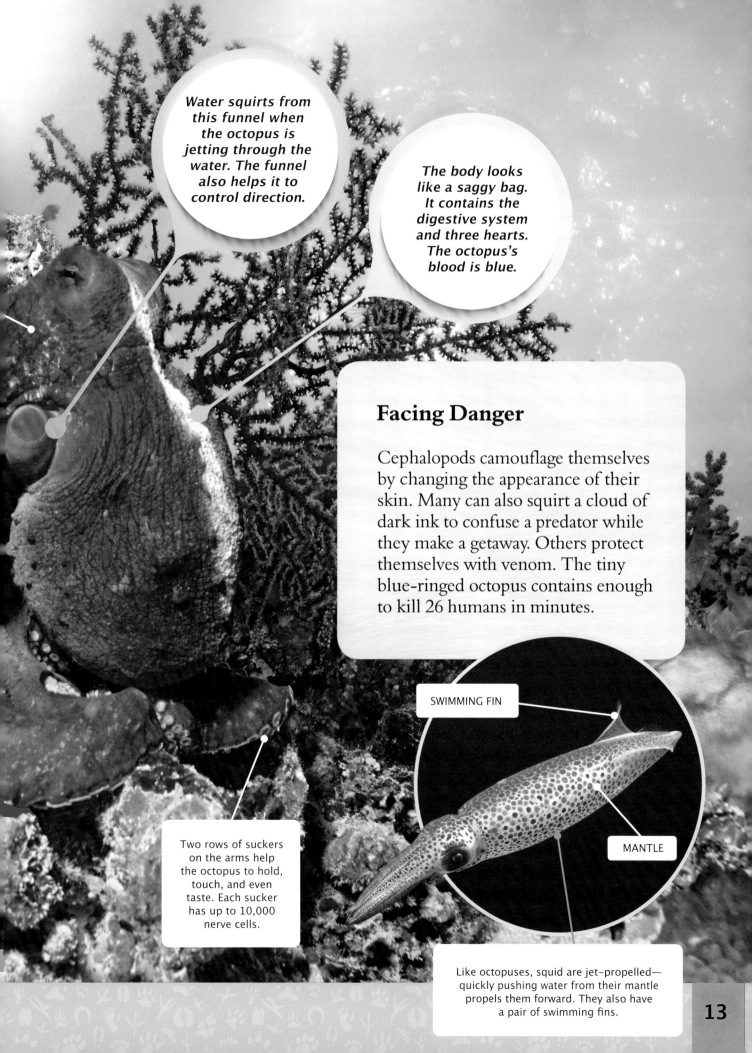

Water squirts from this funnel when the octopus is jetting through the water. The funnel also helps it to control direction.

The body looks like a saggy bag. It contains the digestive system and three hearts. The octopus's blood is blue.

Facing Danger

Cephalopods camouflage themselves by changing the appearance of their skin. Many can also squirt a cloud of dark ink to confuse a predator while they make a getaway. Others protect themselves with venom. The tiny blue-ringed octopus contains enough to kill 26 humans in minutes.

SWIMMING FIN

MANTLE

Two rows of suckers on the arms help the octopus to hold, touch, and even taste. Each sucker has up to 10,000 nerve cells.

Like octopuses, squid are jet-propelled— quickly pushing water from their mantle propels them forward. They also have a pair of swimming fins.

Seahorses

A horse-like head and snake-like tail make seahorses distinctive fish. Together with their close relatives, pipefish and sea dragons, they form a family that contains around 230 species—of which 120 are found in warm, shallow waters off the coast of Australia. They eat tiny crustaceans and are well-camouflaged among plants.

Prehensile Tail

Seahorses are weak swimmers because they don't have the usual tail fin that pushes fish through water. They move by fluttering the small dorsal fin low down on their back. Easily swept away by strong currents, seahorses anchor themselves by wrapping their tail around a plant stem.

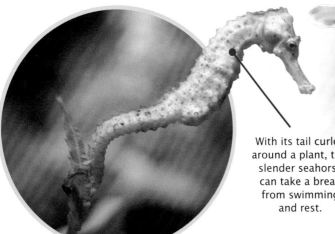

With its tail curled around a plant, this slender seahorse can take a break from swimming and rest.

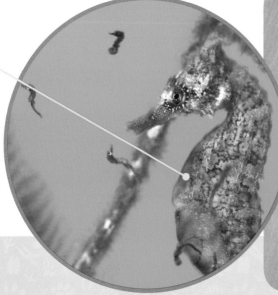

When seahorse babies swim out of their father's pouch they are tiny, but fully formed.

Having Babies

Seahorse fathers give birth! The female lays as many as 2,000 eggs in a pouch on the male's belly. He provides oxygen and nourishment and, after about a month, the eggs hatch. Clouds of miniature seahorses swim off into the ocean. Only about one in 20 of these tiny fry will survive to adulthood.

Sea dragons and pipefish swim horizontally through the water. Seahorses swim upright.

The sea dragon's long, thin snout can suck up thousands of sea lice or other small crustaceans in a single day.

Leafy lobes disguise the sea dragon so it looks like floating seaweed. They don't help it to swim.

LEAFY SEA DRAGON

PHYCODURUS EQUES
"HORSE WITH SEAWEED SKIN"

Habitat: Ocean; South and East Australia
Length: Male 9.8 inches (25 cm); female 7.9 inches (20 cm)
Weight: Male 4 ounces (113 g); female 3.2 ounces (90 g)
Diet: Plankton, small crustaceans
Life span: Up to 10 years
Wild population: Unknown; Least Concern

Crabs and Lobsters

There are more than 60,000 crustaceans, of which more than 6,750 are crabs and 75 are lobsters. Prawns, barnacles, and wood lice are also crustaceans. Crabs and lobsters have ten legs and a tough exoskeleton—their shell—that protects their soft body. Each time they outgrow the shell, they shed it. There is a new, bigger one underneath.

The lobster has two compound eyes (eyes with many lenses) that sense changes in the light. Sight is not as important to a lobster as touch and smell.

The Y-shaped pair of smaller antennae can detect smells.

The long antennae help the lobster to feel its way and sense prey.

The lobster's larger claw is used for crushing prey and battling with other lobsters.

The lobster's smaller claw has a serrated edge. It is used for cutting up flesh.

Land and Sea

Crabs can live in the sea, in fresh water, or on land. Land crabs have to return to the water to spawn (release their eggs). Lobsters are found only in the sea. Both crabs and lobsters are omnivores, feeding on a mix of plant and animal matter.

The blue land crab lives in an underground burrow. It eats leaves, fruits, grasses, and animal foods, including insects and carrion.

Moving House

Hermit crabs are unusual because they don't grow their own shells. They protect their soft body by moving into another creature's abandoned shell. Hermit crabs choose their shell carefully to be exactly the right fit. As they grow, they move into bigger shells.

A hermit crab chooses its shell carefully so that it is a perfect fit. As it grows, it moves into bigger shells.

AMERICAN LOBSTER

HOMARUS AMERICANUS

Habitat: Ocean beds; Eastern North America
Length: 12 inches (30 cm)
Weight: 1.1 pounds (500 g)
Diet: Crabs, mussels, sea stars, other marine invertebrates
Life span: Up to 100 years
Wild population: Unknown; Least Concern

Coral Reefs

Reefs are structures built up from the chalky casings of billions of tiny invertebrates called polyps. They are one of the world's richest habitats, home to about a quarter of all marine life. More than 1,800 species of fish inhabit the Great Barrier Reef.

Hard and Soft

The polyps that build the reef are known as hard corals. When they die, they leave behind stony exoskeletons. New generations grow on top. There are also soft corals on the reef that can look more like plants. Both hard and soft corals form colonies in distinctive shapes. Hard corals have six waving tentacles to catch food; soft corals have eight.

Beneath this living colony of Acropora *coral is stony rock. It formed from the old exoskeletons of dead* Acropora *polyps.*

Gorgonian, also known as the sea fan, is a colony of soft corals. Its flexible fan shape sways with the current. Gorgonian can be red, orange, yellow, pink, purple, or white.

CORAL SPECIES

HARD CORALS	SOFT CORALS
Blue coral	Dead man's fingers
Brain coral	Gorgonian
Bubble coral	Sea mat
Elkhorn coral	Sea pen
Great star coral	Star polyp
Pillar coral	Toadstool coral
Table coral	Tree coral

Reefs teem with life. These sea goldies are shoaling above a reef off the Maldives in the Indian Ocean.

Smaller fish like these attract sharks and other predators to the reef.

Anemones are polyps attached to the reef. Their stinging tentacles catch and paralyze prey. Clown fish stay close to their host anemones.

Amazing Partnership

The reef is a dangerous place. The clown fish stays safe by living among the stinging tentacles of the sea anemone. Unlike most animals, the fish is immune to the anemone's toxins. In return, the clown fish cleans algae off the anemone, brings it food, and clears away any scraps.

The Deep

The deep ocean begins around 656 feet (200 m) below the surface and plunges to more than 6.2 miles (10 km). It is the largest but least explored habitat on earth. It is also dark and cold, and the water pressure is enough to crush an unprotected human. Animals that survive there are highly specialized.

Gulper eels are deep-sea fish with a huge gaping mouth. Their long, eel-like body stretches to accommodate meals of any size.

Deep-Sea Zones

The twilight zone reaches down to 0.6 miles (1 km). Many animals here have huge eyes to make the most of the light. Below this is the dark zone. Around 90 percent of the life here can produce its own light to find the way, communicate, or lure prey.

Birthplace of Life

The first single-celled life forms appeared around hydrothermal vents—holes on the seabed where heat and minerals bubble up from Earth's core. These bacteria survive without energy from sunlight. In turn, they support all sorts of life, including giant tube worms, mussels, clams, shrimp, crabs, and fish.

The 7-foot– (2 m) long tube worms that live by deep-sea vents are simple creatures. They have no mouths, guts, or anuses.

HUMPBACK ANGLERFISH

MELANOCETUS JOHNSONII

Habitat: Deep ocean; worldwide
Length: Male 1.2 inches (3 cm); female 7.1 inches (18 cm)
Weight: Male 1.8 ounces (50 g); female 10 ounces (280 g)
Diet: Fish, marine invertebrates
Life span: Estimated up to 3 years
Wild population: Unknown; Least Concern

Only female anglerfish have a lure. Its glowing tip attracts prey or a mate.

Small fins cannot move the fish through the water at any speed. This ambush predator spends most of its time barely moving.

The humpback anglerfish eats crustaceans, snails, shrimp, and other fish. It can dislocate its jaws to fit in large prey.

Long, sharp, curved teeth can imprison prey unlucky enough to be caught.

Jellyfish

Jellyfish aren't fish—they are invertebrates from the same family as anemones and corals. They have been around for around for 650 million years and live in every ocean. Instead of a brain, a jellyfish has a net of nerves that helps it detect changes in its surroundings and find prey.

Dangerous Jellies

Jellyfish are predators. They eat whatever they can fit into their mouth, including plankton, crustaceans, fish eggs, fish, and other jellyfish. They paralyze or kill their prey with venom produced by cells on their trailing tentacles. They also use their tentacles to push the food into their mouth.

The box jellyfish is the world's most poisonous animal. The stings of some species can kill a person in minutes.

Life of a Jellyfish

Jellyfish have complicated life cycles. Adults gather—sometimes in their millions—in breeding swarms called blooms. They release eggs and sperm into the water. The fertilized eggs must go through four different life stages before they become medusas (adults). Many are eaten and never reach adulthood.

In a bloom, sometimes the bigger jellyfish eat the smaller ones.

Behind the jellyfish trail 24 long maroon tentacles. They have venomous stings.

Four frilly, creamy-white "arms" surround the sea nettle's mouth. Like the tentacles, they have stinging cells.

The main part of the jellyfish is called the bell. The mouth is hidden under the bell.

PACIFIC SEA NETTLE

CHRYSAORA FUSCESCENS

Habitat: Warm waters; E Pacific
Length of tentacles: 9.8 feet (3 m)
Width: 1 foot (30 cm)
Diet: Jellyfish, plankton, other marine invertebrates
Life span: Up to 6 months
Wild population: Unknown; Least Concern

Sea Stars

Sea stars, also called starfish, first appeared in the oceans around 450 million years ago. Today there are around 2,000 species. Most sea stars have five arms, but the largest, the sunflower star, has up to 24. The sunflower star lives in the Pacific and weighs around 11 pounds (5 kg).

Suckers!

The sea star's top surface has scaly skin covered with small spines. Its soft underside is hidden. The sea star clings to rocks or sand using the suction cups at the end of its feet. Even so, fish, crabs, sea turtles, and gulls all hunt sea stars.

On the underside of the sea star's body are hundreds of tiny tube feet. They are used for moving and catching food.

Most of a sea star's major organs are in its arms. It even breathes through its arms—the skin takes in oxygen from the water.

The purple sunstar's skin has protective, scratchy spines. This sea star hunts sea cucumbers, mollusks, and other sea stars.

ELEGANT SEA STAR

FROMIA NODOSA

Habitat: Indian Ocean
Width: 3.9 inches (10 cm)
Weight: 1.2 ounces (35 g)
Diet: Small marine invertebrates
Life span: Up to 5 years
Wild population: Unknown; status unknown

At the end of each arm is a simple "eye"—a cell that can detect light and dark.

The sea star can shed an arm on purpose, to distract a predator. It will regrow.

Coral Killer

The crown-of-thorns starfish is named for the long, thorn-like spines that protect the top of its body. It inhabits coral reefs in the Indian and Pacific oceans and feeds on coral polyps. A single crown-of-thorns starfish can eat its way through 65 square feet (6 sq m) of living coral reef in a year.

The crown-of-thorns starfish's thorny spines are tipped with venom.

Fun Facts

Now that you have discovered lots about different kinds of sea creatures, boost your knowledge further with these 10 quick facts!

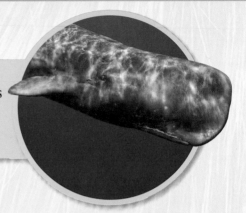

Sperm whales are the world's biggest predators at up to 60 feet (20 m) long. One sperm whale tooth can weigh 2.2 pounds (1 kg).

The ocean sunfish is the world's heaviest fish. Adults can weigh up to 2,205 pounds (1,000 kg).

The Greenland shark is the world's longest-living vertebrate. It can reach nearly 400 years old.

The colossal squid is the world's biggest cephalopod and the largest invertebrate. It is 46 feet (14 m) long and weighs up to 1,650 pounds (750 kg).

The dwarf seahorse is the world's slowest fish. Even at its top speed it travels only 5 feet (1.5 m) in an hour.

The Japanese spider crab is the world's largest crab. Its shell is 16 inches (40 cm) wide and its leg span can be 12 feet (3.6 m) across.

The Great Barrier Reef is more than 1,400 miles (2,300 km) long and can be seen from space. It is the biggest structure built by living creatures.

The deepest part of the ocean, the Pacific's Mariana Trench, goes down 36,070 feet (10,994 m). It could swallow Mount Everest with 1.3 miles (2.1 km) to spare.

Jellyfish bodies are 95 percent water. When jellyfish get stranded on a beach they quickly dry up and disappear!

Once a sea star has pried open a clam, it turns its own stomach inside out and pushes it inside the shell to digest the clam's soft body parts.

Your Questions Answered

We know an incredible amount about the creatures that populate our planet—from the deepest oceans to the highest mountains. But there is always more to discover. Scientists are continuing to find out incredible details about the lives of marine animals, from their life cycles and migrations to how they hunt and survive. Here are some questions that can help you discover more about these amazing water-bound creatures.

Why does the octopus have three hearts?

Most animals—including humans—have one heart. Its job is to pump oxygen-rich blood around the body, and return oxygen-poor blood back to the lungs. But octopuses have three hearts. All three are specialized, and help keep up a steady supply of oxygen-rich blood throughout the animal's sprawling body. Two hearts are solely responsible for transporting blood to and from each of the two gills. The third supplies the internal organs with blood.

When octopuses swim, their organ heart stops beating, so they usually prefer to "crawl" across the ocean floor.

What makes the seahorse a fish?

Apart from very few exceptions, fish are vertebrates that are cold-blooded, live in the water, use gills to breathe, and have bodies that are covered in scales. Although the seahorse does not look like most fish, it does fit all of these criteria. And, like most bony fish, it even has a swim bladder—an organ that helps the animal stay at a certain water depth without having to swim.

How do corals multiply?

In order for corals to spread, they need to create offspring, just as any other organism would. Corals do this in one of two ways. Some create clones of themselves—either a polyp divides when it reaches a certain size, or a small chunk of a colony breaks off in order to form a new colony. Other corals create offspring through fertilization. Once a year, all the corals in an area that are the same species spawn, releasing eggs and sperm that combine in the water to form new life.

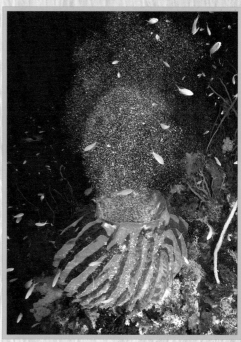

When a coral spawns, it looks like dust clouds are being released into the ocean.

Can sea stars swim?

Sea stars cannot swim; instead, they have a very unusual way of moving through the ocean. The underside of each of their arms is lined with hundreds of tiny tube feet. Each tube is filled with seawater and is used to move the sea star's body across the ocean floor. Not only do the tube feet move the sea star quite quickly, they also help it hold its prey, such as clams and mussels.

How do animals see in the deep ocean?

While the parts of the ocean that are close to the surface are well-lit, anything below 3,280 feet (1,000 m) depth has no visible sunlight at all. But animals living in these virtually lightless areas still need to see in order to mate, hunt, and survive. Their eyes have adapted to seeing only those parts of the light that can travel in this darkness. This means they pick up even the smallest amounts of light to great effect. A lot of animals in the deep sea also use bioluminescence to communicate—they emit light that is produced by their bodies.

Many creatures in the ocean, including jellyfish, use bioluminescence to communicate.

Glossary

camouflage To blend in with one's surroundings.

cephalopod A marine mollusk with a large head and eyes and a ring of tentacles that have suckers.

cold-blooded An animal that doesn't keep its own body warm, but rather heats it with the help of its environment (for example by basking in the sun).

crustacean An arthropod with two-part legs and a hard shell.

exoskeleton A hard, outer skeleton.

filter feeder An animal that eats small creatures by filtering them out of the water.

fin A flattened body part of an animal used for swimming.

fish A cold-blooded vertebrate that only lives in the water. It has gills and fins.

gills Slits in the side of an animal's body that help it breathe underwater.

invertebrate An animal that has no backbone.

omnivore An animal that eats plants and meat.

oxygen A gas that is essential for life.

plankton Microscopic plants, algae, and animals that float in the oceans.

poison A substance that can damage or kill a living being if injected or swallowed.

predator An animal that hunts and eats other animals.

prehensile tail A tail that is able to hold or grasp.

prey An animal that is hunted and eaten by other animals for food.

school A large group of fish.

spawn To release eggs.

thrust The force that moves something forward.

toxin A substance that can harm or kill a living being.

venom A chemical that is injected into another animal to paralyze or kill.

vertebrate An animal that has a backbone.

Further Information

BOOKS

Broom, Jenny, and Katie Scott. *Animalium*. Somerville, MA: Big Picture Press, 2014.

MacQuitty, Miranda. *Shark*. New York, NY: DK Children's, 2014.

Rockett, Paul, and Mark Ruffle. *Ten Thousand, Eight Hundred and Twenty Endangered Species in the Animal Kingdom*. Chicago, IL: Heinemann-Raintree, 2016.

Savage, Stephen. *Focus on Fish*. New York, NY: Gareth Stevens Publishing, 2011.

Woodward, John. *Ocean: A Visual Encyclopedia*. New York, NY: DK Children's, 2015.

WEBSITES

Ducksters: Fish
www.ducksters.com/animals/fish.php
Head to this website to find out all there is to know about fish.

Natural History Museum: Oceans
www.nhm.ac.uk/discover/oceans.html
This webpage offers lots of video clips and the latest ocean news from around the world.

Index